Prof. FRANK S. LEWIS
January 1906

THE NEW SCIENCE

Weaponless Defense

===

Edited and Published by

PROF. FRANK S. LEWIS

438 S. Spring St.

LOS ANGELES. CALIFORNIA

===

Illustrations by

PROF. LEWIS, TOMMY BURNS, heavy weight boxing
champion, and WILLIAM V. GREGORY,
middle weight wrestler

Originally published 1906,
By FRANK S. LEWIS

Copyright 2010
MartialHistory.com
ISBN 978-0-557-65509-0

IT is the mission of this volume to present clearly and concisely as complete a system of WEAPONLESS DEFENSE as possible. Being well aware of the difficulty of teaching this art on paper, I will endeavor to use a simplicity of language than can be readily understood, relying on the style and number of engravings to give the student a good knowledge of how to protect him or herself against one or more assailants, armed or otherwise, without having to resort to the use of a weapon. Also how to protect a friend from assault or from himself, as the case may require.

THIS KNOWLEDGE put into practice throughout this broad land would undoubtedly, every day, result in the prevention of some case of murder or manslaughter, justifiable or otherwise, and will leave the sunshine in many and many an honest home that would otherwise forever be blotted out by the hasty act of some father, son, or brother, who if they do not suffer the death penalty, will go to prison as the result of their hasty actions and the too convenient revolver or knife.

It is the boasted advertisement of the revolver manufacturer that his weapon makes all of one size. SO DOES SIX FEET OF EARTH. Think of the loss to the world every day through deaths, and the sorrow incurred though the use of this evener of size, and then the facts will come home to you that what is required is a universal knowledge of this GREAT WEAPONLESS DEFENSE.

WHAT IT CONSISTS OF.

WEAPONLESS DEFENSE is an exact science comprised of the two great defensive sciences, Boxing and Wrestling. It is Boxing and Wrestling combined. It is so arranged that you can oppose a blow with a fall, in the same time that the Boxer would take to counter. If you throw an adversary to the floor you have much more advantage than if he remained standing. Besides the majority of the holds render an opponent powerless to offer resistance. It also permits your hitting your opponent when opportunity occurs. The good Boxer is "up against it" when he gets in a street fight with the good Wrestler. Yet both are at a decided disadvantage. The Wrestler is liable to receive a bloody nose or a discolored optic before he succeeds in securing his hold on a good Boxer. This once done, however, there is only on result, the Boxer is at the mercy of his more sturdy opponent who can easily force submission. On the other hand, if the Boxer has a practical knowledge of the high falls and leverage holds taught in the NEW SCIENCE, he should readily defeat the Wrestler, and it he Wrestler has acquired a knowledge of Boxing, they would be on an even footing. So you see that a thorough knowledge of the NEW SCIENCE makes one man equal to two good ones, and two good ones, along these respective lines, would do much execution in an uneducated crowd.

The Japanese claim that one Jiu-Jitsu expert can defeat several men. If so the NEW SCIENCE expert should be able to defeat several more men, as he has the added advantage of being a good Boxer.

THIS SCIENCE also teaches how to disarm an assailant, how to take away a stick, knife or revolver, without injury to yourself or any one else, except some discomfiture to the assailant. It also teaches how and where to locate the weak spots in an opponent's body, where a blow or sudden pressure will have most effect. But most important is the knowledge of leverage that the pupil acquires. You secure a hold in such a way that you make you opponent work on the short end of the lever, while you have the long end. Thus the little man with a good knowledge of THIS DEFENSE is more than the equal of the Giant without it.

Many of those leverage holds are most important to the Police or other officers, and if known by them the unpleasant practice of clubbing some unwilling victim into submission will be avoided.

Many of the carrying holds will be found useful to the fire laddie in handling helpless people, whilst making descents with them down ladders or other dangerous places, or to the ambulance corps in carrying invalids or insensible people.

THIS DEFENSE also teaches methods of vivification by which a person can be brought back to consciousness in the shortest time possible.

BOXING.

HISTORY tells us that the Jewish Patriarchs were the very first to encourage Boxing. Human nature is nothing if not aggressive, and even the Jews, always the most peaceable of people, had taken to reducing their numbers by the use of the knife, to such an extent, that the Chiefs introduced Boxing as a method to settle their family *imbroglios* and save their lives. That the art prospered with the Jews is plain, as they were the first to introduce it into England, and even today the Jews are amongst the very first exponents of the art in this country.

The Anglo Saxon and the Celt, with their natural love for fair play and desire for bloodless warfare, soon took up the Jewish system of settling their disputes, and Boxing prospered under their patronage to such an extent that it was placed under rules, and competitors often boxed for prizes. These rules were known as the London Prize Ring, and this marks the era of ring champions. Later the rules were modified and called after the Marquis of Queensberry, a noted patron of the sport. They still bear his name and are yet in use.

The English introduced Boxing into this country, where it is greatly appreciated and receives the most liberal patronage and we hold, practically, all of the Boxing Championships.

WRESTLING.

WRESTLING is one of the oldest sports known to antiquity. It was an art amongst the ancient Egyptians. Plates found on Homer's tomb illustrate over three hundred different positions which would be "Catch as Catch Can" style of today. In the days of Rome's greatness Plutarch asserts that Wrestling was given first place in the three Gymic games, namely Wrestling, Boxing, and Foot-racing. It is generally supposed that the Romans introduced it into England. But it is safe to say that Wrestling like Boxing, in the noble, manly and humane practice of the sport, is of Saxon, Celtic and Gallic origin. Like Boxing, the English introduced Wrestling into this country, and to a knowledge of Wrestling and Boxing in the education of our youths, the practice of which strengthens the mind and body and builds up a manly courage, that makes them disdain to resort to atrocities as practiced by other nations amongst whom these sports are unknown, to that practice we owe much of the noble courage that elevates the English speaking people, and which stern, impartial and logical minds must recognize as the proudest attribute of our AMERICAN CHARACTER.

AS AN EXERCISE.

The practice of the NEW SCIENCE is the finest, possible. Every muscle of the entire body is brought into play. It cultivates grace, activity, endurance and strength. And the practice not only improves and develops the muscular system, but regulates the functions of the organism and refines the senses, giving greatly increased strength, steady nerves and cheerfulness. It is a most interesting study, as it requires a greater amount of judging than any other branch of athletics. It is also the greatest possible developer of hardihood, courage and cool determination.

In entering upon the practice of the NEW SCIENCE the following suggestions will be found beneficial. Secure, if possible, the services of a competent instructor, if not in your locality, get an active even tempered companion as near your own height and weight as possible. Provide a set of good boxing gloves, also a good gymnasium or lawn tennis shoe. Assume your proper position on guard, look your opponent squarely in the eye and avoid showing by an expression of the face or glance of the eye when or where you intend to hit or clinch. Keep the eyes open and the teeth firmly closed, breathing through the nostrils. Never bit the lips or put the tongue between the teeth. Never drop the hands unless out of distance. in practice do not repeat the same movement twice in succession. Do not be impetuous, try to out general and out point your opponent. Science is superior to strength in this respect. If you drop science and rush in, strength will surely win. Never lose your temper, cool courage is superior to hotheadedness.

Never break into a rough, unmeaning scramble. Be manly and seek no undue advantage.

Figure 1

Correct boxing position, as shown in Figure 1. Stand with the feet from twelve to sixteen inches apart, to suit the height. The left toe pointed in a direct line with your opponent. Left knee vertical with the instep. Right heel in line with, and behind the left heel. The toe turned slightly out. The body should be held erect, inclined a little forward. The left arm should be held so that the left elbow passes free and easy by the hip, the forearm pointing in a direct line to your opponent's face, thumb on top and closed down over the first knuckles of the first and second finger. This rule also applies to closing the right hand. The right hand should be carried so as the heel of the hand covers the pit of the stomach, and be held open except when striking a blow. Both elbows should be kept as closely to the sides as possible. The position of the head is very important. The chin should be held well in, and the face turned partly to the right, so as not to bring both eyes in a line with your opponent's left hand. Hold the head so that it may be rapidly thrown to either side to avoid a blow.

This is one of the most advantageous methods of avoiding a blow when countering. It is known as head slipping. There is the slip to the right to counter with the left hand at either face or body. And the slip to the left to counter with the right hand at either face or body. Another movement of the head is called ducking. It consists of dropping the head straight down, to avoid either a left or right hand swing. At the same time countering with either left or right swings to body. You should never duck without hitting, as by so doing you are in danger of your opponent's upper cut. In practice the movements of the arm should be light and free. Never cramp the muscles or compress the hands unless the blow reaches the mark aimed for. Extra tension of the muscles only serve to render the blow slow and tire the arms. Cultivate speed in delivery, make the hand reach the part aimed at in the straightest possible line without any intermission of time between the thought and the blow. Make the most of the weight of the body in preference to using the strength of the arms. Always endeavor to get your blow home. A sure lead is the best protection. Always hit with the back of the hand. In delivering a straight left hand lead to the face, have the thumb on top. In delivering a left hand to the body have the finger nails turned down. In delivering a straight right to the face or body have thumb on top. In delivering swings, to either head or body, have the finger nails turned down. The same in delivering a right hand cross counter. When delivering upper cuts have the finger nails turned up and in.

FOOT CHART.

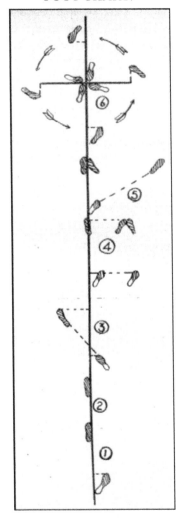

Figure No. 1 illustrates the correct position of the feet when standing on guard.

Figure No. 2 illustrates the step forward to deliver a left hand blow. Be sure to keep your right toe on the floor when hitting.

Figure No. 3 illustrates the step in and to the left to deliver a right hand blow.

Figure No. 4 illustrates the slip to the right to avoid your opponent's rush or lead. First move your left foot about sixteen inches to the right, following with your right. Then quickly face your opponent by pivoting on your left toe, as shown in Figure No. 6.

Figure No. 5 illustrates side-stepping. Move your right foot about twenty inches to the right, at the same time shifting the weight of your body over your right leg allowing your opponent's lead to pass. Immediately resume boxing position by swinging on the toes facing your opponent.

Figure No. 6 illustrates pivoting or circling, which means to keep facing your opponent, no matter what position he assumes. To do so keep moving to the left, if possible, thus avoiding his right hand. Keep the weight of your body poised over your left leg, move the right foot the necessary distance to the right, pivoting on the bail of the left foot. It is well to practice the circling by quarters, being sure to have your feet come in correct boxing position every time. Then practice making the circle in two movements, this will teach you to face your opponent quickly and correctly after avoiding his rush, by either slipping or side-stepping. One cannot get too much foot practice. Good foot work is essential to become an expert in the new science.

Figure 2

Figure No. 2 shows the guard for the left hand lead to the face. To form this guard correctly, raise the arm with the open palm turned out until you can see your opponent's eyes over your wrist. Hold the elbow well down, catching the blow either on the palm of the hand or the fleshy part of the forearm, lifting it up and out.

Figure 3

Figure No. 3 shows the left hand guard to a right high blow to the face. To form this guard correctly, raise the arm with the open palm turned out until you can see your opponent's eyes underneath your wrist. Hold the elbow well down and catch the blow on the fleshy part of the forearm, lifting it up and out.

Figure 4

Figure No. 4 shows how to guard a left lead to the body. To form this guard correctly, slightly raise the elbow and turn the palm of the hand down and out, catching the blow either on the wrist or fleshy part of the forearm, turning it down and out.

Figure 5

Figure No. 5 shows the guard for the right hand lead for the body. To form this guard correctly, slightly raise the elbow, turning the palm of the left hand down and out, describing a small half circle. Catch the blow on the palm of the hand or wrist, turning it down and out.

Figure 6

Figure No. 6 illustrates what is known as a straight left hand counter at the face. To form this movement correctly, use the right high guard as illustrated in Figure No. 2, at the same time step in and deliver a straight left hand at your opponent's face.

Figure 7

Figure No. 7 illustrates the right hand counter at the face. To form this movement correctly, use the left high guard as illustrated in Figure No. 3, at the same time stepping in and delivering a straight right hand blow at your opponent's face.

Figure 8

Figure No. 8 illustrates what is termed straight left hand counter at the body. To form this movement correctly, oppose your opponent's left lead with your right high guard, and stepping in, deliver a straight left hand blow to the pit of the stomach.

Figure 9

Figure No 9 illustrates what is known as the right hand straight counter at the body. To form this movement correctly, oppose your opponent's right high lead with your left high guard, stepping in simultaneously and delivering a right hand blow to the pit of the stomach or heart.

Figure 10

Figure No. 10 illustrates the duck and left hand counter at the body. To form this movement correctly, duck down and to the right, allowing your opponent's lead to pass over your left shoulder, simultaneously delivering a blow to his body with your left hand. In making this delivery turn the finger nails down, allowing the elbow and shoulder to reinforce the strength of the arm.

Figure 11

Figure No. 11 illustrates the duck and right hand counter at the body. To form this movement correctly, simultaneously with your opponent's left lead, move your left toe about fourteen inches to the left, allowing his blow to pass over your right shoulder. At the same time delivering a straight right to the body.

Figure 12

Figure No. 12 illustrates a right hand cross counter. To form this movement correctly, simultaneously with your opponent's left high lead, head slip by turning your face to the left and inclining your head over your left shoulder. At the same time moving the left foot about twelve inches to the left and delivering a right hand blow outside of his arm at his jaw or neck. Great care must be taken in the delivery of this blow. If you swing it you are liable to break your hand on the top of your opponent's head. The proper way is to start the blow with the thumb up, when the hand has reached the height of your shoulder turn the finger nails down, causing the hand to corkscrew around your opponent's arm and land flush on his jaw or neck.

Figure 13

Figure No. 13 illustrates a left hand inside counter. To form this movement correctly, simultaneously with your opponent's left high lead, head slip by inclining your head over your right shoulder. Step in and deliver straight left at your opponent's chin. This blow can be followed up by a right hand cross counter as your opponent withdraws his arm, move your foot to the left suddenly.

Figure 14

Figure No. 14 illustrates a right hand counter, commonly called the inside cross. To form this movement correctly, simultaneously with your opponent's left high lead turn your face to the left and move the left foot about fourteen inches in the same direction, delivering a straight right hand to your opponent's face.

Figure 15

Figure No. 15 illustrates the left hand upper cut. To form this movement correctly, when your opponent inclines his head forward step in and deliver a left hand lifting blow to his chin. This blow can be used as a counter to an opponent's lead by stepping to either side as the case requires.

Figure 16

Figure No. 16 illustrates right hand upper cut. To form this movement correctly, step inside of your opponent's left lead and deliver a right hand lifting blow to the chin. Upper cuts may also be used to the body effectively if your opponent is in a bent forward position.

Figure 17

Figure No. 17 illustrates left hook to the jaw. To form this movement correctly, having feinted your opponent into extending his left hand or drawing back his right, step in suddenly and deliver a short half arm swing to the jaw with your left. Be sure and turn your finger nails down in the delivery of the blow.

Figure 18

Figure No. 18 illustrates right hook to the jaw. To form this movement correctly, having feinted your opponent into drawing back his left hand, step in suddenly and deliver a short half arm swing with your right to his jaw, being sure to turn your finger nails down in the delivery of the blow.

Figure 19

Figure No. 19 illustrates left hand hook to the body. To form this movement correctly, simultaneously with your opponent's left high lead, duck to the right, allowing his blow to pass over your left shoulder. Deliver a short left hand swing to the stomach.

Figure 20

Figure No. 20 illustrates a right hook to the body. To form this movement correctly, duck under your opponent's right high swing, step in and deliver a short right swing to the pit of the stomach.

Figure 21

Figure No. 21 illustrates an extension block to right hand cross counter. Having feinted your opponent into an attempt to cross counter, suddenly move your left hand out, catching him on the arm, just above the elbow. You now stand ready to counter his intended cross with a hard right to the face or body.

Figure 22

Figure No. 22 illustrates a left hand cross guard. When your opponent delivers right hand blow at your head, incline the body slightly backward allowing his blow to fall short. At the same time striking him on the outside of the arm with your left hand. This has the effect of throwing him off his position and leaving him open to a hard right hand blow at the face or body.

Figure 23

Figure No. 23 illustrates another left hand cross guard. When your opponent makes a straight left hand lead at your face, oppose it with the palm of your left hand striking his forearm just above the wrist, pushing it over your right shoulder. Simultaneously step in and deliver a hard right hand swing to the spleen or kidneys.

Figure 24

Figure No. 24 illustrates right hand cross guard. Oppose your opponent's left hand lead at the head with the palm of your right hand, pushing it over your left shoulder. This has the effect of throwing him open and leaving you in position to deliver a hard left hand blow at the face or body. By simultaneously advancing the right foot you perform what is known as the left shift, thus adding increased strength to the blow.

Figure 25

Figure No. 25. Avoid your opponent's left lead by head slipping, at the same time step in and to the left with your left foot. Place the palm of your left hand on your opponent's right hand or forearm thus pinning it to his body. You now stand ready to deliver a hard right hand cross counter to your opponent's jaw as he withdraws his arm.

Figure 26

Figure No. 26. Oppose your opponent's left lead the same as in the previous exercise, simultaneously pinning his right hand with your right hand. You now stand ready to deliver a hard left hook or swing to his jaw.

Figure 27

Figure No. 27 illustrates what is known as the heart blow. When your opponent leads at your face with his left hand, lift his left arm with your left hand, stepping in deliver a hard right hand blow over the heart.

Figure 28

Figure No. 28 illustrates a chop to the kidneys.

Figure 29

Figure No. 29 illustrates a kidney blow. Avoid your opponent's left lead by head slipping, at the same time stepping in with your left foot, simultaneously delivering a hard right swing to the kidneys. Have your finger nails turned down.

Figure 30

Figure No. 30 illustrates what is known as slipping. Head slip your opponent's left high lead by turning your face to the right and bending the body slightly forward, simultaneously move your right foot about fifteen inches to the right, following it with your left. This has the effect of letting your opponent go by, immediately pivot on the ball of the left foot, facing him in his new position. This movement can be used effectively to avoid a rush or get out of a dangerous corner.

Figure 31

Figure No. 31. Avoid your opponent's right high swing by swinging your body to the right and backwards, shifting your weight onto your right foot. This has the effect of making his blow fall short, and it leaves you in position to deliver a hard right hand return at his face or body before he can recover.

Figure 32

Figure No. 32 illustrates what is known as the safety block. This position is seldom used except when you are in a dazed or worried condition. Whilst in this position it is almost impossible for your opponent to deliver an effective blow.

Figure 33

Figure No. 33 illustrates the safest method of coming out of a clinch. Grasp your opponent's arms from the insides just above the elbows push back on his elbow, straightening your arms, you can then step away safely and resume your boxing position.

Figure 34

Position Attention

Figure No. 35 illustrates a very simple and very effective throw. When your opponent strikes at your face with his left hand, oppose the blow with your right high guard, as in figure two. Simultaneously draw your right hand back, grasping his wrist securely, suddenly step forward grasping him in the arm pit with your left hand. At the same time placing your left foot on his left foot, your heel on his instep and toe turned out,

Figure 35

now give a sudden pull bringing his left hand down past your right hip, at the same time swinging your body sideways. This will have the effect of throwing him over on his back. If his blow should be delivered with his right hand, raise your left high guard, and advance your right foot, the fall is just the same except the positions are reversed.

Figure 36

Figure No. 36 is a continuation of No. 35. If your opponent is exceptionally strong or heavy, and you anticipate trouble in pulling him over, as you give the pull drop to your right knee. This will have the effect of tossing him over your left leg with ease.

Figure 37

Figure No. 37. When your opponent draws his right hand back to strike, suddenly step in, grasp his left wrist with your right hand, placing your left on his left shoulder or collar. At the same time advance your right foot. This has the effect of carrying your head over his left shoulder, thus avoiding his blow.

Figure 38

Figure No. 38 illustrates the finish of the throw. Having secured position as in figure No. 37 suddenly strike your opponent on the back of his leg with your left heel, simultaneously pulling down and in on his left arm and shoulder. When practicing this with a friend be very careful as the fall is very sudden and severe.

Figure 39

Figure No. 39. When your opponent draws back his left hand to strike, step in suddenly, striking him a hard back hand blow with your left hand or wrist across the jaw or neck, simultaneously striking his left heel with your left toe. This is known as the cross trip and the suddenness of the movement makes it a very effective fall. The same fall can be made by using the right hand and right foot to strike and trip.

Figure 40

Figure No. 40. When your opponent strikes at
your face with his left hand, avoid the blow by
ducking to the right under his arm. At the same
time advance your right foot and grasp his right
elbow with your left hand, thus avoiding his blow
and placing you in a position for the throw as
illustrated in Figure No. 41.

Figure 41

Figure No. 41. Now grasp your opponent around the left thigh from behind, being sure to retain your hold on his right elbow, lift and throw forward on his head. This is known as the crotch and elbow throw.

Figure 42

Figure No. 42. When your opponent swings at your head with his right hand, duck to the left under his arm, at the same time advancing your right foot outside of his left foot, grasping him around the waist with your right arm and by the knee with your left hand. Lift and throw over on his head and shoulders. This is known as the cross buttock, and is a very dangerous fall. Be very careful in practice.

Figure 43

Figure No. 43 illustrates a back buttock. Avoid your opponent's left lead by ducking under his arm to the left, as illustrated in Figure No. 10. From this position step or jump behind him, being sure to keep your left foot in advance of the right, and simultaneously grasping him around the waist with your left arm. Now lift him across your left hip, as shown in this Figure. Be careful in practice, as this is a very high and dangerous throw.

Figure 44

Figure No. 44 illustrates the manner of avoiding your opponent's lead and ducking in to secure a leg hold.

Figure 45

Figure No. 45. When your opponent leads or swings at your head with either hand, suddenly bend forward, catching him in the stomach with your head and grasping him around the knee with both hands. Lift and throw backwards.

Figure 46

Figure No. 46. Suddenly step in, grasp your opponent's collar with your left hand and his left thigh from the inside with your right hand. Lift up on the leg and press back his head with your left forearm against his throat. Throw backwards.

Figure 47

Figure No. 47. Avoid your opponent's left high lead by ducking under his arm to the left, at the same time stoop low, grasping him back of the left instep with your right hand and the right thigh, with your left hand. Place your left foot behind his right heel. Push and throw backwards

Figure 48

Figure No. 48. This is what is known as the stiff knee lift. Duck in close under your opponent's high lead simultaneously grasping him in the crotch with your left hand and placing your right hand against his knee. In making the lift, keep your back straight and you can easily throw your opponent over your shoulder, or by pulling on the leg cause him to fall on his back.

Figure 49

Figure No. 49 illustrates what is known as the crotch and arm lock. Grasp your opponent's left hand or wrist with your right hand. Duck in, and under his left arm, grasping him around the left thigh from the inside. Pull down on his arm with your right and lift with your left. In this position you can easily lift an opponent twice your weight. You can now either throw him backwards over your shoulder, or forward onto his back, as you choose.

Figure 50

Figure No. 50 illustrates the front chancery and bar lock. It can be used as a very effective block and throw against your opponent's attempted leg hold. Shoot your right arm up underneath your opponent's left arm, placing your hand well across his back and high up as possible. At the same time grasping him around the head with your left arm. From this position you can easily twist him over on his back.

Figure 51

Figure No. 51 illustrates the saddle lock. Suddenly step in under your opponent's right lead or swing. Bend low, shooting your right arm well up into his crotch and grasping him around the small of the back with your left arm. Lift and throw backwards.

Figure 52

Figure No. 52 illustrates another dangerous back throw. Having secured your opponent's right wrist in your left hand, suddenly duck under the arm. Secure his other wrist in your right hand. From this position straighten up and throw him over your back. If you cast his wrist loose at the proper time he is bound to fall on his head. Be very careful in practice.

Figure 53

Figure No. 53 illustrates the side chancery hold. As shown in the illustration this can be used as a choke hold, and belongs to the family of strangle holds.

Figure 54

Figure No. 54 illustrates the chancery and hip lock. Having secured your opponent's head, as in Figure No. 53, suddenly step in with your right foot, placing your hip underneath his body. Lift and throw forward. This is a very effective fall.

Figure 55

Figure No. 55 illustrates the break for the chancery hold. When your opponent secures your head, as in Figure No. 53, grasp his right wrist with your right hand, straighten up as much as possible, reach up with your left hand, grasping him by the forehead. Pull on his head and arm. This will effectively break the hold. If you continue to pull back on your opponent's head and retain your hold on his wrist, you will force him to turn round in front of you. This accomplished, you will find you have secured a hammer lock from the front and front chancery on your opponent.

Figure 56

Figure No. 56 illustrates the front hip lock. Having gotten into a side position with your opponent, grasp him around the body with your left arm and his left wrist with your right hand. Place your hip in front of him. Lift and throw him forward on his head.

Figure 57

Figure No. 57 illustrates the back hip lock. Having secured holds as in the previous illustration, suddenly place your left hip behind your opponent. Raise up his left arm. Lift and throw backwards.

Figure 58

Figure No. 58 illustrates a break for a body hold. When your opponent rushes in and grasps you around the body with both hands, grasp his right elbow with your left hand and his right collar with your right hand. Press the forearm against his throat thus forcing his head back and causing him to loosen his arms.

Figure 59

Figure No. 59. Having succeeded in breaking your opponent's body hold, retain your hold on his arm, swing in sideways, placing your right leg behind him. Pull on his arm, throwing him over your leg sideways. This is known as the flying roll, and is a very effective fall. The same fall can be taken when your opponent makes a high lead with either hand.

Figure 60

Figure No. 60 illustrates an effective break for the body hold when your opponent has succeeded in lifting you off your feet. Place your right hand underneath your opponent's chin and your left on top of his head. Twist and push backward on his head. If a fall is made, you will land on top.

Figure 61

Figure No. 61 illustrates the head twist. Suddenly step in between your opponent's hands, place your left hand on top of his head and your right under his chin, give his head a sudden twist and push backwards. If your opponent does not fall backwards, this movement will have the effect of making an opening for a good hold. It is also a certain break for a body hold.

Figure 62

Figure No. 62 illustrates one of the numerous ways of securing the back hammer lock. When your opponent delivers a left high lead, avoid it by stepping to the right. At the same time raising your left high guard. Grasp your opponent's wrist with your left hand and his elbow with your right hand. Pull down on the wrist and push up on the elbow. Simultaneously stepping behind him. Now push his hand up his back between the shoulders. This is one of the most effective holds in wrestling, and if forced causes great pain. It is easy to force submission with this hold.

Figure 63

Figure No. 63 illustrates another method of securing a hammer lock. When your opponent uses a high lead, suddenly grasp his wrist with both hands. Hold the arm up and circle underneath it. Retain your hold and force his hand well up his back. If you hold the wrist tightly the arm receives a peculiar twist that causes severe pain and probably dislocation. Be very careful in practice.

Figure 64

Figure No. 64 illustrates yet another method of hammer locking. Suddenly grasp your opponent's right hand with your right, across the back, bending his hand down and in at the wrist, simultaneously grasp his right elbow with your left hand, with your thumb on top and the two first fingers pressing in on the nerve just above the "funny bone." Push back on the hand and up on his elbow, and you will be surprised how easily you can force submission.

Figure 65

Figure No. 65 illustrates the hammer lock and half Nelson hold. Having secured the hammer lock by the methods described, secure the half Nelson by pushing your hand up underneath your opponent's free arm, placing the hand on top of his head. Pull down on the head and push up on the hammered arm, and you will easily force him over on to his back.

Figure 66

Figure No. 66 illustrates another method of going behind your opponent which is known as the drag hold. Quickly grasp your opponent's left wrist with your right hand and his left elbow with your left hand, giving him a sudden pull to the left and by you. At the same time step behind him with your right foot.

Figure 67

Figure No. 67 illustrates a fall taken from the drag hold. Having succeeded in going behind your opponent, retain your hold on his left elbow, grasp his other arm at the elbow and either place your foot against his or strike him back of the knee with your knee, at the same time lurch your body forward. This movement will have the effect of throwing him on his face and leaving you in a position to secure any of the submission holds.

Figure 68

Figure No. 68 illustrates the wrist half Nelson and hip lock. Having passed behind your opponent as described, secure his right wrist with your right hand and the half Nelson with your left hand. Now place your right hip in front of him. Lift and throw. This is a very dangerous fall as he has no way of protecting himself. Be very careful in practice.

Figure 69

Figure No. 69 illustrates the double Nelson. Having passed behind your opponent, quickly reach up under both arms and lock your hands on the back of his head. By stepping to one side and pulling down on his head you can force him over on to his back. This hold is considered so severe that it is barred in all amateur mat contests.

Figure 70

Figure No. 70. This is almost a similar fall, and is secured in the same way as Figure No. 67, except that you place your foot in front of your opponent's throwing him over your leg onto his face.

Figure 71

Figure No. 71 illustrates a blow at the base of the brain. Having avoided your opponent's left lead by stepping to the right, grasp his arm with your left hand, holding it on your left shoulder, simultaneously deliver a right hand blow with the knuckles on the back of your opponent's neck. Be careful in practice, as this blow often renders your opponent unconscious.

Figure 72

Figure No. 72. Quickly grasp your opponent's right wrist with your right hand, lift his hand up high and secure a half Nelson with your left hand. Hold your left arm stiff and pull down on his right across your arm. Be sure and keep the palm of his hand turned up. You can now force him to walk along quietly.

This hold is a valuable one to the police officer.

Figure 73

Figure No. 73 illustrates the arm and cross collar hold. This hold is secured in exactly the same manner as the preceding one, except that you grasp your opponent's collar high up with your left hand. This is by far, the most convenient of the police holds.

Figure 74

Figure No. 74. This is known as the Japanese "Come Along." Grasp your opponent's left hand with your left hand, hold it in front of you with the palm turned up. Now, wrap your right arm around his left arm, grasping your left wrist. This has the effect of keeping his left arm straight, and by pressing down on the hand, you can induce him to accompany you without much parlance.

Figure 75

Figure No. 75. This is probably the most common police grip used. The different methods of obtaining it are explained in Figures No. 62, 63, and 64. Having secured the hammer lock, hold it with your left hand and grasp your opponent's shoulder with your right hand. This prevents him from turning round and by lifting up on his hammered arm, you can force him to walk along peaceably in front of you.

Figure 76

Figure No. 76. Secure the hammer look, by the method described in Figure No. 64. Having pushed your opponent's arm behind him, hold it in that position with your right hand, and push your left arm up under his right forearm with your hand on top of his shoulder. You can now release your right hand, holding it free for emergencies and by retaining the pressure upward on his arm with your left, can force him to move along in a hurry.

Figure 77

Figure No. 77. This illustrates a very pretty and effective throw. Avoid your opponent's left high lead by ducking to the right, at the same time advancing your right foot. Grasp your opponent by the left instep with both hands, quickly lift up his foot behind, tossing him forward on his face.

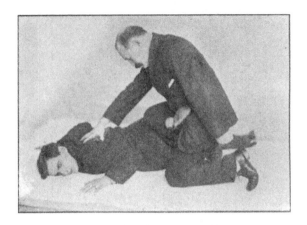

Figure 78

Figure No. 78. Having thrown your opponent forward on his face, as previously described, retain your grip on his foot and step over it with your right leg. Now, by dropping on your left knee you secure a left hammer lock as illustrated. In this position there is no release for your opponent. Be very careful in practice, as it is an easy matter to dislocate the knee or hip. By grasping your opponent's head and pulling him sideways whilst in this position, the spine can be dislocated.

Figure 79

Figure No. 79 illustrates another submission hold. Having thrown your opponent on his back by any of the falls previously described, drop quickly with your right knee on his left arm at the elbow, simultaneously pinning his right arm at the same place. You can easily hold him as long as necessary, or beat him into submission, as the case requires.

Figure 80

Figure No. 80 illustrates another method of holding, or forcing submission. Having thrown your opponent forward on his face, quickly drop with your left knee back of his right shoulder. Grasp him by the right wrist with your right hand twisting his hand with the palm up. Use your knee as a lever, pull up on his arm and press down on his head. Any of the last three holds will be found useful in preventing insane persons from doing injury to themselves, or others.

Figure 81

Figure No. 81. This is what is known as Garrotting, and is chiefly used by thugs to choke a victim into insensibility. It is secured by stepping up behind, and encircling his throat with the right arm pulling his head backwards, simultaneously placing the left hand on the back of his head and grasping the left wrist with the right hand. Now, by pulling down on his victim's head with his left hand, and backward with his right arm, the thug's object is soon accomplished. To avoid this hold, turn quickly to the left, striking your opponent a hard right hand blow in the stomach. To break the hold after it is secured, pull in your chin, swelling out the muscles of the throat, thus easing the pressure on the windpipe. Simultaneously reach up with your left hand, grasping the fingers of your opponent's left hand, grasping the fingers of your opponent's left hand, pulling them away from your head and breaking them if necessary.

Figure 82

Figure No. 82 illustrates another hold used by the thugs or hold-up men to render their victim powerless whilst their accomplice goes through his pockets. It consists of stepping up from behind and quickly grasping him around the body, over his arms.

Figure 83

Figure No. 83 illustrates how to release yourself from the preceding hold. Finding yourself grasped in the manner described, inflate your lungs and set the muscles of the chest and back to their utmost capacity. This will have the effect of stretching your assailant's arms as much as possible. Now suddenly exhale and relax the tension of the muscles, making your chest as small as possible. Simultaneously dropping down on one knee, grasp your assailant's wrist with your right hand and his collar with your left. Bend forward, throwing him over your head.

Figure 84

Figure No. 84 illustrates the straight-arm-lock. If you expect an attack from behind, this hold can be used effectively by grasping your assailant's arm as he passes it over your shoulders. The hold once secured, the result is inevitable. This fall can also be used to oppose either of the high leads at the face.

Figure 85

Figure No. 85 illustrates the front hammer lock. When your opponent raises his right hand, grasp his right wrist with your left hand and his right elbow with your right hand. Push up and back on his wrist and pull on his elbow, forcing his hand back over his shoulder. By releasing your hold on his elbow and pushing your hand up behind his arm, grasping either your own or opponent's wrist, you have secured what is known as a bar on a hammer. Now, by exerting very little strength you will either throw your opponent on his back or dislocate his arm.

Figure 86

Figure No. 86 illustrates a method of taking away a knife from an assailant. When your assailant raises his hand to strike a downward blow, quickly step to the left so as to avoid the stroke, should you miss his arm. Grasp his right wrist with your right hand and his right elbow with your left hand, pushing up and back on the wrist and pulling in on the elbow, thus forcing his hand back over his shoulder. Should this not cause him to drop the knife, put on the bar with your left hand, as described in No. 85. See Figure No. 88.

He must now either drop the knife or suffer a broken arm.

Figure 87

Figures No. 87 and 88 illustrate the method of taking away a stick from an assailant and the ensuing fall. Which positions are fully described in No. 86.

When practicing taking away an assailant's gun, knife or stick, be careful that the gun is not loaded and the knife is not sharp so as to avoid accidents. Should your assailant strike a blow sidewise at your head or shoulder with the stick,

Figure 88

instead of down, as illustrated in Figure No. 87, duck under it, as illustrated in Figure No. 44, and secure a leg hold, or as in Figure No. 42, and throw him on his head with a cross buttock. Or else rising quickly grab his arm at the elbow and the stick near his hand and try for the hammer-lock, as illustrated in Figures No. 62 or 64, and you can easily take the stick away from him.

Figure 89

Figure No. 89 illustrates one method of taking a revolver from an assailant. If he has drawn his weapon and raises his hand to shoot, step in quickly grasping his wrist with your left hand and his elbow with your right. Push his arm straight up, at the same time grasping him around the neck with your right arm. By pressing his arm back you can force him to drop the revolver or hold him until assistance is rendered.

Figure 90

Figure No. 90 illustrates another method of taking your assailant's revolver, as he draws his weapon from his belt or hip pocket, step quickly to the side of his gun arm, grasp his hand firmly by his wrist with your right hand, bending it in, simultaneously push your left hand through from behind inside of his arm, grasping the gun around the cylinder, pulling in and backwards. This will force him to release his hold and leave the weapon in your possession. The same method may be used to take a knife from an assailant, except that you grasp his hand with your left hand instead of the knife.

Figure 91

Figure No. 91 illustrates the manner of avoiding a kick from your assailant and the ensuing fall. When your assailant is about to kick with his right foot, quickly step to the right advancing your right foot. Grasp his right leg about the instep with your left hand and his left collar with your right hand. Now, kick him on his left leg back of the knee with your right foot, and the fall is accomplished.

Figure 92

Figure No. 92 illustrates another manner of avoiding your opponent's right kick. Quickly move your left foot about twenty inches to the left, allowing him to kick up under your left arm. Step in, grasping his right leg around the knee with your left hand and his left shoulder, with your right hand. Step on his left toe with your left foot, pulling him over on to his head. Still another method of avoiding a kick is to step quickly backwards, allowing his foot to pass up in front of you. Grasp his heel with both hands and lift up, throwing him backwards.

Figure 93

Figures No. 93, 94, 95 and 96 illustrate the manner of lifting and carrying an insensible person out of danger. Figure 93 illustrates the first part of the lift. If lying on the floor, place the person on their back, then stepping astride the body, grasp them around the body underneath the arm-pits, raising them to a sitting position. Now

Figure 94

make the lift to position illustrated in Figure No. 94. Hold the person in this position with your left arm whilst you release your right hand grasping them by the left wrist. Raise their left arm over your head as illustrated in Figure No. 95. Now pull on the left arm holding them in this position whilst you place your left arm around their left

Figure 95

thigh from the inside. You now have assumed the position of the crotch-and-arm lift and it is an easy matter to raise them across your shoulders. Having accomplished this, change their left wrist from your right to your left hand, as shown in Figure No. 96. You now have them securely tied on your shoulders and can easily carry them any reasonable distance. You also have your right

Figure 96

hand free to open doors or assist you out of a window or down a ladder as the case may require.

STUDY AND PRACTICE.

Students of the NEW SCIENCE should take up the boxing end first. Study well the chart on footwork and get all the practice possible on those movements. Then proceeding to the blows and guards, take up each movement separately and repeat them until you can perform each lead and guard correctly without hesitation.

In leading, pay special attention to distance and the correct position of the hands when delivering blows.

In guarding, always have the hands open, being sure to turn the palms in proper position, thus meeting your opponent's arm or fist in the shortest possible time.

Having mastered the leads and guards, the next practice should be stopping and countering. "The Stop" is a blow delivered as an opponent prepares to lead. Stops are invariably executed with the left hand to your opponent's chin or shoulder. Watch him closely, and just as he makes some movement or expression that causes you to believe him about to lead, shoot out your left hand hard, beating him to it, as it were. In stopping a blow, guard the face with the right hand and draw the stomach well in. A boxer's success depends largely on his ability to counter. In order to hit hard it is necessary to excel in this branch of the science. The student should practice the counters separately, avoiding his opponent's leads by the guards or head-slips, as shown in the engravings.

Being sure to time his deliveries so as to reach his opponent before he has recovered from the impetus of his lead, thus making a counter-blow doubly hard.

FEINTING. No one can become a good boxer who cannot feint successfully. Feinting is deceiving. The key-note of successful feinting is rapidity and decision. To feint, step in with the left foot about six inches, following it up with the right, partially straighten the left arm, as in leading at your opponent's head or body, quickly retract the movement with the muscles relaxed. Then step in from eight to twelve inches, and deliver the left lead like a piston rod to any unguarded part of your opponent's face or body. Feinting is also used to open up your opponent's guard. When you desire to send the right to the face, feint low with the left. Your opponent will naturally seek to block this blow and in so doing will leave an opening for your right hand at his face. If you desire to send the right to the body, feint high. This will have the effect of causing your opponent to raise his right high guard, leaving his stomach exposed to your right hand blow. Should your opponent try to counter your feint with his left hand, slip to the left, delivering a right hand body counter, as described in Figure No. 11. Feints can be made particularly useful in drawing leads from your opponent when he would rather remain on the defensive, thus giving you a chance to use any of the counter blows. Oftimes a slight forward movement of the shoulder, accompanied by a forward movement of the head will serve to draw your opponent's lead.

You can easily change a feint into a delivery without drawing back the arm. For instance, when you feint at your opponent's face with your left hand, have the thumb on top. As your opponent raises his right high, guard, quickly turn your finger nails down, turning the feint into a blow at his stomach and backing it up with the weight of your body.

This movement can also be reversed by feinting your opponent's body with the finger nails turned down, and quickly turning the thumb on top, your blows will reach your opponent's face, without you even changing your glance. Another feint, which I have used effectively on an opponent who manifested a willingness to cross-counter, was to offer a left lead at his face, striking a few inches short, at the same time leaving my right guard low to draw his counter, and quickly moving my left hand, stop the intended cross counter, as illustrated in Figure No. 21, meeting him with a straight right hand to the face. A successful feinter invariably uses considerable footwork, stepping in and out, to the right and to the left, keeping the hands continually in motion. You should observe care in keeping an even balance, so as to facilitate speedy recovery.

In practicing the different holds that lead to a throw or submission, it is well to start by opposing the high blows with falls. Have your opponent deliver a straight left hand lead fairly at your face, practice opposing it by the different methods described, until you can do so surely and without hesitation. Then proceed opposing the right hand lead in the same manner. It is a splendid practice for the student to work against an experienced boxer, in doing so, study out different methods for guarding and avoiding every assault he may make. Having him repeat them over and over again until you know how to meet them automatically, and if possible gain a submission hold every time. Also study out plans of attack that will lead up to securing submission. In practicing, study out as many variations as possible, and practice each one thoroughly. The position to assume while waiting the assault of an opponent depends largely upon what you expect him to do. I have given one I call "position attention" as shown in Figure No. 34. If your opponent is a boxer, this position will be found handiest, as you have to guard yourself against blows. If, however, your opponent shows an inclination to grapple with you, I would assume more of a wrestler's position, with the hands lower down, your body squared more to the front and feet kept apart enough to keep it well braced. But close enough together to be able to side-step or step forwards or back easily. Never get caught with your feet close together. Keep your hands open and held in such a manner that you can guard any part of your body, strike a blow or clinch with your opponent, as the occasion requires. You should practice feinting in this position as much as in boxing. For instance, feint to strike your opponent a high blow, but instead, quickly stoop down and secure a leg hold. Or having feinted to draw his lead, quickly duck under it and to either side and secure a hold from behind. Practice is the only thing which will make you an expert in those maneuvers. It is impossible for an instructor to map out any set course of attack and defense that will work well in every instance.

STRATEGY is also one of the effective attributes of the new art. Of this, the instructor can impart very little. The student must work it out for himself. The knowledge is acquired by study and practice with different opponents. For instance, if you are attacked by a party who shows a superior knowledge of boxing, but is hard to induce to lead, step in suddenly and kick him on the shins with either foot, this will have the effect of making him drop his hands, giving you an opening for either a blow or hold. Other tricks that might be resorted to would be to throw your cap in your opponent's face, or stepping in quickly, grasping him by the lapels of the coat, throwing it back over his shoulders, thus pinning his arms. It is my opinion that the man who becomes an expert in the NEW SCIENCE and possesses a good knowledge of strategy is practically invincible of any number of untrained or indifferently trained opponents!

THE MOST EFFECTIVE BLOWS, those generally tried for by experienced boxers, are the point of the chin, on either side, under the ear, or juggler blow, the solar plexus or pit of the stomach, the heart blow, spleen blow, and kidney blow. Of those, the first four will produce unconsciousness, and sometimes have proven fatal. The spleen and kidney blows are not so dangerous, but result in the wearing down of the opponent. In addition to these blows, is the blow on the collar-bone, which may break it. The blow on the Adam's Apple which may cause injury for life. The blow at the back of the neck which may cause death. The blow across the base of the spine which may also cause death. A blow delivered simultaneously on both ears is also extremely dangerous. A blow delivered on the nerve center underneath the upper arm above the elbow, either with the side of the hand or the knuckles will disable that member, as will also a blow across the biceps. A blow delivered at the base of the brain, when your opponent assumes a crotch position or bends forward to secure a leg hold, is very apt to result in unconsciousness.

There are many places where pressure exerted on the nerves or blood vessels will assist in forcing submission. But only a few that are practical for use. For instance, pressure with the thumb or forefingers on the inside of the wrist in the location of the pulse will effectually deaden the hand. Pressure of the thumb on the back of the hand between your opponent's thumb and fore-finger, accompanied by the bending in of the wrist will force your opponent to open his hand. Pressure exerted by the fingers underneath your opponent's arm just above the elbow will assist in hammer-locking. Pressure can also be used on the jugular vein just below the ear, which will have the effect of bending your opponent's head forward. Pressure exerted on the wind-pipe will result in strangulation, and sometimes death.

VIVIFICATION.

As previously mentioned, many of the blows are capable of producing a dangerous state of unconsciousness. When the victim does not regain consciousness in a very short time and the heart action and breathing reach a low point, vivification should be resorted to.

Immediately disrobe the victim sufficiently to facilitate his breathing. Raise him to a sitting position, pass your left arm around his chest and press it, at the same time striking him gently with the palm of your hand over the spine at the region of the seventh rib. The pressure and the blow should be given as the victim exhales. It has the effect of stimulating the pneumogastric nerves and aids in the contraction and inflation of the lungs and the action of the heart. As he begins to show signs of consciousness, call his name loudly thus stimulating the auditory nerves.

Should more effective means of respiration be required, stand behind the victim. Press your thumbs deeply into his shoulders near the neck just at the pectoral arch where the clavic and scapula meet. Extend the fingers of each hand over the shoulders in front to aid in applying the pressure. While doing this also kick the victim's back over the third from the last vertebrae. These two actions should prove effective.

A small round mouthed bottle filled with absorbent cotton saturated with ammonia, or a bottle of smelling salts held under the victim's nose as he inhales will clear his head and greatly assist in restoring consciousness.

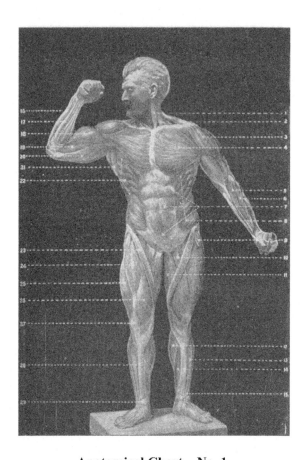

Anatomical Chart—No. 1.

SEE OUR GUARANTEE ON LAST PAGE.

KEY TO CHART 1.

1. Sterno-cleido-mastoid.
2. Trapezius.
3. Deltoid (or shoulder).
4. Pectoralis major.
5. Extensor carpi radialis.
6. Extensor communis digitorum.
7. Rectus abdomis.
8. External oblique.
9. Tensor faseiae femoris.
10. Pectineus.
11. Abductor longus.
12. Gastronnemius (or calf).
13. Tibalalis anticus.
14. Plexor longus digitorum.
15. Extensor longus digitorum.
16. Plexor carpi ulnaris.
17. Plexor Carpilradialis.
18. Biceps (or front arm).
19. Brachialis anticus.
20. Triceps (or back arm).
21. Latissimus dorsi.
22. Serratus magnus.
23. Sartorius.
24. Rectes femoris.
25. Vastus externus.
26. Vastus internus.
27. Patella (or knee pan).
28. Tibia (or shin bone).
29. Annular ligament.

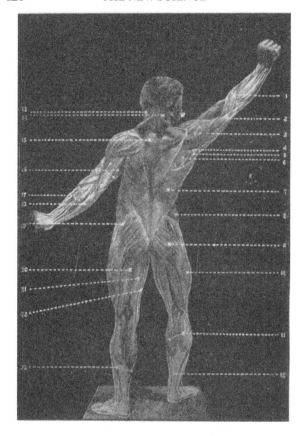

Anatomical Chart—No. 2.

SEE OUR GUARANTEE ON LAST PAGE.

KEY TO CHART 2.

1. Supinator longus.
2. Triceps.
3. Deltoid.
4. Teres minor.
5. Teres major.
6. Infra-spinatus.
7. Latissimus dorsi.
8. Posterior portion of external oblique.
9. Gluteus maximus.
10. Vastus externus.
11. Gastrocnemius.
12. Tendon achillis.
13. Sterno-mastoid.
14. Splenius capitis.
15. Trapezius.
16. Triceps.

   Extensor carpi radialis longior.

17. Extensor carpi radialis brevior.

   Extensior communis digitorum.

18. Extensor carpi ulnaris.
19. Gluteus medius.
20. Riceps.
21. Semi-tendinosus.
22. Semi-membranosus.
23. Soleus.

The Lewis School

OF

Physical Training

A SQUARE DEAL

Our Square Deal Contract : : : : : :

438 South Spring Street

If after sixty days Conscientious Trial under our Instructions, you do not feel fully benefitted and compensated for the outlay, we agree to refund your entire membership fee.

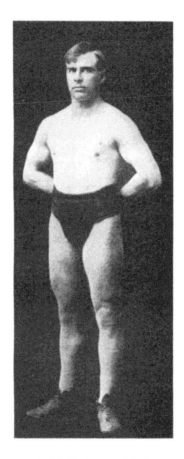

WM. V. GREGORY
3 month's reduction 45 1bs.

CHRIS PERSON
A month body building 42 lbs.

EARLY DEATH IS MERELY A BAD HABIT.
DO NOT GET THE HABIT.

Live to be at least one hundred years old. As a matter of fact we each have the free will to create our own longevity to a great extent, if we can only muster faith enough to persuade ourselves to properly train our minds and bodies.

I am forty-four years old myself, and have devoted the greater part of my life to promoting health, both in others and myself. I am absolutely convinced that I can live to be one hundred years old and do things worth doing to the very end.

If it were not that nature's laws ordain that a time must come when decay will take place in the body more rapidly than repair can offset the destruction, it would be possible, generally speaking, for man to make himself immortal in this world, through the right amount and kinds of exercise. By proper breathing of pure air, sensible diet, proper use of water inside and out and the right amount and quality of clothing. By those aids man is so well able to prolong his life to a healthy and advanced old age, that it may well be said that health and longevity is optional.

But the greater amount of people pay but little heed to the subject and are content to get along "any old way," trusting to reach old age with a fair average of health, success and GOOD TIMES. My system of Physical Training will make all those things possible and assure a long life.

A NATURAL TREATMENT FOR DISEASE.

My Perfected System of Physical Training Makes Exercising a Positive Pleasure. What it Consists of.

Internal Vibration for vitality and lung power.

Flexing or double contraction for strengthening and increasing the size of the muscles.

Calisthenics, or Stretching Movement, principally selected from the "setting up" exercises of the American and British Army and Navy.

ABDOMINAL EXERCISE, for strengthening the stomach and abdomen and reduction of weight.

Few instructors in gymnasiums and other physical culturists seem to be able to differentiate between the development of muscle proper or muscle fiber and the development of muscle energy, with the result that after persistent and steady effort of months, one wonders that the expected results are not forthcoming; notably the enlargement of the muscles which is rightly considered a sure sign of progress.

With nearly 20 years experience in all-round athletics, fully 10 years of which I have been instructing, and during which time I searched diligently for a system of exercises which would bring desirable and lasting results, testing all that was on the market, including apparatus work; it was not until I combined the tension system with calisthenics that my search was rewarded, the solution of which is simple.

The author's back from a photograph taken in 1891 showing a muscle bound condition.

SEE OUR GUARANTEE ON LAST PAGE.

The muscular system of the body is made up of antagonistic or opposing muscles; that is for every movement made there is a muscle, or set of muscles, to bring about a correspondingly opposite movement.

The tension system does not involve the use of any apparatus whatever. It consists in antagonizing the muscles; making them oppose each other throughout the different movements. When this is done the muscles involved in the separate movements are made tense, and by adding increased resistance to the muscles from day to day as strength is gained, the tension system enables the perfect application of this increased resistance. But the tension system has great drawbacks, in that it produces undue hardening of the muscular tissues, and a muscle-bound condition results if it is used exclusively. In my system, which is an adaptation of the tension system and calisthenics. these drawbacks of the tension system are effectually overcome, and its greatest possibilities realized—possibilities it does not possess or approach when used alone.

The quick, light calisthenic movements, without any tension whatever, taken alternately with the tension movements, stretch the muscles and keep them perfectly pliable, as they must be in order to make possible perfect muscular control and insure perfect circulation of blood. By this combination you get a natural system of physical culture. The tension system develops the size of the muscles and muscle energy, and the calisthenic movements produce in the muscles pliability and beauty of outline, giving in addition grace and speed of movement.

PHYSICAL TRAINING TOO OFTEN STRAINING.

I am very careful to see that my pupils do not overdue. I am afraid there is more straining than training in the systems most in vogue. It is altogether a too common impression that physical training's whole mission is to create large, knotty muscles, and the ability to perform feats of strength that are out of the ordinary. The majority of pupils are liable at first to endeavor to build up great shoulders and arms. This is wrong, as it is done at the expense of the lungs and heart.

A permanent strength cannot be built up from the outside, not until the lungs, heart and solar plexus are practically perfect, should you look at your biceps.

BREATHING.

As there can be no bodily development of the highest kind until the pupil has learned to breathe correctly, the chest should get the first attention. Correct breathing should be taught at the very first or in connection with calisthenic exercises.

Correct breathing exercises increase the size power, flexibility and symmetry of the chest walls, and the voluntary muscles employed. They also increase the function capacity of the involuntary muscles, and promote health and strength to the entire body by quickening circulation and increasing respiration.

Nobody with perfect control of the pectoral and abdomal muscles die of consumption; and to cure it the first essential is to restore and maintain proper respiratory action.

Tuberculosis cannot progress in a properly active lung, through which the blood circulates freely. People in the early stages of consumption are often sent to high altitudes to effect a cure; not that the mountain air has any more curative properties than the valley air, but it is so rarified that the patient must breathe quickly and deeply in order to live. Now, this enforced breathing opens the air cells and increases the circulation which cures the disease. If the patient would stay in the low altitude and breathe in the same manner, the cure would be much more speedy and certain. But why think of the cure? Use the preventative, learn those systems and practice them.

SOLAR PLEXUS SYSTEM.

In order to lay the foundation for a long life, a great deal depends on getting the Solar Plexus to properly behave.

Most people first learn of the Solar Plexus as through Bob Fitzsimmons who won the heavy weight championship by landing a hard hook on that portion of Corbett's anatomy, thus causing him to suffer untold agony and forcing him to remain down and out for the count.

But why? Well this. There is more about the Solar Plexus than most people ever found out. Fitz, and Corbett included.

It is the "Abdominal Brain," and controls the sympathetic or involuntary nervous system which has a whole lot to do with the emotions, and when you get it working properly, (instead of kicking), with the heart and lungs also in good condition, then a long and happy life is assured.

The definition of a plexus is a network of either nerves or veins, the seat of the solar plexus being the "pit of the stomach." It is composed of the epigastric nerves, motor and sensory, sending off branches to the heart, lungs, throat and larynx. Those nerves in a state of health are the best of servants. If diseased, they become the most despotic of tyrants and make life miserable, and long life impossible for their slave owners.

BELLIE WELL, ALL WELL, is the reasoning of "wise John Chinaman," as his question relative to a friend's health would imply, How's your bellie? This shows the yellow man's wisdom, as 90 per cent, of all sicknesses are centered in the belly. This knowledge has led me to complete a set of special exercises that I term MY SOLAR PLEXUS SYSTEM, with which I am having phenomenal results. Cases of dyspepsia, constipation and indigestion of long standing, are disappearing in from seven to twenty-one days, and the cure in every instance has been permanent. Besides, these exercises are a positive preventative from rupture, and often effect a cure even in bad cases.

SECURE THE PREVENTATIVE AND PRACTICE IT. LEARN THOSE EXERCISES.

OBESITY CURED BY A SIMPLE FORM OF TREATMENT.

Oh! That this too solid flesh would melt. Thousands of people are repeating Shakespeare's lament every day. Not only because of the uncomfortable feeling, but also of the knowledge that an unusual gain of flesh is as dangerous as an unusual loss of weight. There are two general forms of Obesity; one in which the fat is quite evenly distributed over the body, head and limbs; the other in which the superfluity of fat is principally in the region of the abdomen.

There are also exceptional cases where other parts of the body are abnormally developed; each requiring different treatment principally.

I wish to assure you that I do not pretend to do anything impossible when I claim to cure or remove this disease positively and permanently. I have had years of experience and investigation in reduction, and have compiled a set of simple exercises which will certainly do the work in each instance. I am not inclined to be egotistical, yet I do not favor false modesty. I have studied and practiced a number of advertised methods for reduction of weight, and whilst some were good, yet the results were invariably the same, namely, when you quit using the exercise and returned to your regular style of living, the fat returned also.

Cut II

DIFFERENT WHEN USING MY SYSTEMS.

I have reduced persons weighing 250 pounds, to 200 pounds, in four months; persons weighing 220 pounds, to 190 pounds, in two months. I can reduce your weight from ½ to 1 pound per day, until you have reached the weight desired; then you retain the weight because the exercises that you do in reducing, set up the chest and so harden the muscles of the abdomen that they will remain so, also assuring an erect and graceful carriage of the body.

I give you no severe rules to follow as regards eating or drinking. I do not lace up the body in bandages or trusses. Your exercises, instead of being violent, become a positive pleasure after a few trials. They are adapted to persons of every age or sex. Everyone gets my careful personal attention.

Cut I

SKIN BATHING AND MASSAGE.

There are three necessities toward a healthy skin, namely, sweating, friction and bathing. The skin is composed of two layers, the cuticle, or epidermis, and the cutis or derma, which form the inner and outer layers, respectively. The outer layer consists of flattened, dry scales, the thickness of which differs in various portions of the body. The inner layer, whilst dense, is also tough and yielding, and under its surface is found a numerous supply of blood-vessels and nerve fibers.

Skin diseases are mostly all due to internal causes. One can readily see the seat of trouble is inside, before it comes in evidence on the skin. Deeply imbedded in the dermis are the sweat glands. Those tubes are about a quarter of an inch in length, the inner ends closed. They coil in globes something like a sixteenth of an inch in diameter At the back of the neck there are about four hundred of those sweat glands to the square inch, while the palm of the hand contains about twenty thousand. The sweat, itself, is made up of moisture composed of salts, and urea which is the most important waste product of the body. The skin also depurates about one-fiftieth as much carbon oxide as the lungs. This shows the necessity of exposing the skin to the air and sunlight.

A direct relation between the skin and kidneys can be noted by the fact that the more perspiration there is on the skin, the less fluid is eliminated by the kidneys. Conversely, then, when the kidneys are very active, there is not much perspiration. Exercise, therefore, is of direct benefit to the kidneys, insomuch as it relieves those organs of much of what would otherwise be their work.

We can easily understand that normal health is impossible unless the skin is healthy. I always look to the skin as an infallible index of the health of the pupil. True, there are pretty skins possessed by diseased people, but there is the rosy, healthy skin which shows the perfect man or woman underneath. The touch of the skin is a sure indication of the state of health. If the skin be properly rosy, reasonably moist and warm, soft and elastic, then I know that I have under my observation a normally healthy skin.

The first essentials are nourishment by the proper foods. Next, exercise bringing profuse perspiration, thus vigorously eliminating waste matter, frequent bathing in order to remove this waste matter accumulated on the surface of the skin. Friction caused by rubbing the skin with a coarse towel or the hand, should be resorted to in order to rub off the dead tissue, which should be taken with the dry skin. Food, water and air must be regarded as the great chemical agents that benefit all parts of the body as well as the skin. Whilst exercise is the great physical agent that sets in motion all of those chemical agents and insures perfect and sound health.

BATHING.

Outside of its sanitary objects, bathing stimulates the functions of the skin, and also produces a stimulating or sedative effect upon the body. Baths are of various temperatures, either cold, tepid, warm or hot. Cold baths are used as a stimulant after a moderate amount of exercise. Care should be taken, however, as harm is often done by this practice. If not accustomed to the cold bath, I advise that you begin by taking the chill off the water but finish, invariably. with a cold shower. Hot baths are used erroneously by some people, and have ruined many healthy skins, as it causes the skin to become inactive, and washes out all of the natural oil. By eliminating hot baths, and having baths first tempered in harmony with the natural warmth of the body, after exercise, the skin can be improved fully as much as the muscular development.

Personally, I give all my pupils advice on bathing as the case requires.

MASSAGE is also a great benefitter and beautifier of the skin. I am an enthusiast on this branch of the healing art, and have always made a careful study of it. I believe that, especially when taken after exercises, its value cannot be overestimated. Alone, it is good, but not so beneficial as after a work-out. It is the rest after the work, and replaces, not only broken down tissue, but a few additional ones, each time, and forces the process of recuperation by increasing the flow of fresh blood (to the part massaged), through the capillary walls so as nutriment can be absorbed by the muscles. Another benefit of manipulations, is to remove the waste or worn out tissue, much more thoroughly than would be accomplished by the heart, unaided. A fatigued muscle will be rested better by five minutes massage, than after two hours rest. A thorough massage of the body is the equivalent of four hours refreshing sleep, as it carries off fatigued products, thus resting the tired parts, and forcing the process of recuperation. It also relieves the congestion of such internal organs as the brains, lungs, intestines, uterus, kidneys, etc., by increasing the flow of blood to those parts, and stimulates, directly, the nervous system, by increasing the activity of the involuntary muscles, and so relieves various functional derangements.

PROF. F. S. LEWIS.

A FEW WHO HAVE TESTED THE SYSTEM; WHAT THEY THINK.

Prof. F. S. Lewis:

Dear Prof.—We, your pupils, take great pleasure in recommending your System of Physical Training. It has in every instance been most effective in building up our muscles and reducing or increasing our weight as the case required. Our strength has increased three-fold; whilst the improvement in our breathing and in the condition of our stomachs is wonderful. The exercises are so varied that they never become monotonous, and we look forward to each succeeding lesson with pleasure. On the whole, the improvement we have made, and the benefits we have derived, have far exceeded our fondest expectations. Count us among your boosters.

Gratefully yours,

Signed by 100 members, among them many prominent Business and Professional men of Los Angeles and vicinity.

SEE OUR GUARANTEE ON LAST PAGE.

WRITE FOR CHART OF OUR PERFECTED SYSTEM.

SEE OUR GUARANTEE ON LAST PAGE.

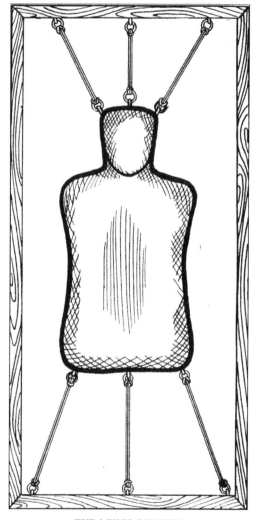

THE LEWIS DUMMY

WRITE FOR CHART OF OUR PERFECTED SYSTEM.

SEE OUR GUARANTEE ON LAST PAGE

The Los Angeles Record of December 26, 1905, says: Young Corbett is getting to be a glutton for work. When he showed up at Prof. Lewis' gym Christmas afternoon, he only intended to work half an hour, as he was not feeling much like work. Lewis set him to punching the bag and skipping the rope, aud before he had enough, an hour had slipped by. He then put on the gloves with Lewis, Terry Davis and a local boxer by the name of Green and spent 45 minutes more.

Prof. Lewis is looking after his condition, and with such a competent man in charge the ex-champion should go to the post in fine condition on the night of the battle. Lewis has the reputation of always being back of the winners. Every man he has trained in the local field has been returned a winner. All have entered the ring in fine condition.

Lewis trained Tommy Burns for his fight with Hugo Kelly and Burns was as fast as lightning that night. Burns went to the post in his fight with Twin Sullivan without the benefit of Lewis' experience and training, and he put up a miserable contest. It is safe to say that he will have Young Corbett in fine condition for his battle and the Denverite will have no excuse to offer on that score if Herrera beats him.

SEE OUR GUARANTEE ON LAST PAGE.

THE GLOBE, LOS ANGELES, CAL., MONDAY, JULY 16TH, 1906:

WHERE THEY BUILD WEAKLINGS INTO STRONG MEN OF ABILITY.

Scientific Secrets Taught in the Lewis School Save Skeptics.

A WEAKLING has no place in this world. He is a drag on the market—a pitiful, helpless thing that is either carried or tossed aside by the strong men who daily cope with battle after battle in the commercial, scientific and professional world.

THE REWARDS of a weakling's life are either pity, contempt, hatred or abhorrence. He is too weak to help himself or others.

THESE FACTS were most vividly impressed on our minds, while visiting the "Home of Strength," an institution that deserves the recommendation and endorsement of every man of affairs.

WHAT INTENSIFIES the interest in this institution is the recent action of Prof. Lewis, who challenged the Cocopah Indian giant, a colossal bulk of flesh and muscle, weighing 400 lbs., to wrestle for a side bet of $1000.

LEWIS, in spite of his 45 years, is a perfect specimen of manhood. He has been following athletic sports since he was 18. For 14 years he held the middle weight wrestling championship, during which time he won over 400 matches and engaged in 63 glove contests, winning 53, drawing 4 and losing 6. Lewis has thrown 10 husky men inside an hour. Later he has been engaged as Physical Director with many of the leading clubs in the principal cities of this country.

WHAT ARE YOU going to do when out walking with a lady: A ruffian comes along, tries to insult you both or hold you up?

Then what would you do if in a public or isolated place you were suddenly brutally attacked? Or suppose you had employer's interests to look after and some fresh young man insisted on running the place without authority? Or providing you were opposed physically in the transaction of your business, what in the world would you do when you did not know how?

NATURALLY THESE MENTAL QUESTIONS came up while carefully investigating the LEWIS SCHOOL OF TRAINING, and there was the complete answer, for it was soon learned that this school is not in existence for the purpose of turning out professionals, but to so develop the student as to enable him to protect himself and friends wherever he may be. When a man is in this condition, he is naturally better able to cope with the world's struggles no matter where he be. His physique gives self-confidence, aids him to generate energy, and best of all, he fears no man, which is a most essential feature of business success and a result of the Lewis course of instruction.

WHEN YOU ENROLL among the Lewis School students you are given a thorough physical examination by Prof. Lewis, who first notes whether you are in shape to take training, and then specially points the required course of development.

YOU ARE MEASURED immediately, and the dimensions of your neck, shoulders, chest natural, chest inflated, thighs, calves, arms and hips are recorded.

When you finish a three months' course, in which perfect satisfaction is guaranteed, it will be a surprise to note an increase from one inch up in the dimensions of the neck; shoulders 2½ and up; chest natural 2 to 3 inches; chest inflated 2½ to 4; thighs 1½ calves ¾ to 1½; arms 1 inch up and down, and hips reduced or increased according to physique.

AT PRESENT there is an average of 100 working members, who in three months learn enough to take care of themselves for life.

ONE OF THE most natural treatments for disease is a course in this muscle building academy, in which every muscle of the body receives proportionate attention.

THE CUTTER FIGHTING department is one of the most interesting in which the art of self-defense is taught without any weapon of defense, which Prof. Lewis terms "weaponless defense." Prof. Lewis teaches the famous Anglo-Saxon "jiu-jitsu." If every respectable gentleman in the United States were to take a course in this alone, crime would be reduced to a minimum.

When studying at the Lewis School of Physical Training you ward off sickness and cure some of the most complicated troubles.

PROFESSIONAL AND BUSINESS men come to the academy at all hours that suit their convenience.

THERE IS NOTHING GRANDER in this large world of ours than strong men—men who have the force to back their convictions.

AN INSTITUTION that builds such men, should at all times command the admiration and respect of every progressive individual in the world.

SEE OUR GUARANTEE ON LAST PAGE.

THE PERFECT MAN.

By Rev. J. S. Trimmer, Rector of St. George's in the
Pines, Helmetta, N. J.

The perfect man is a full-grown man physically. It is
worth while to be full-grown. Saul was chosen King
because of his physical make-up. Daniel Webster
commanded attention because of his magnificent
proportions. When he was in London a certain
nobleman likened him to "a steam engine in breeches."
One of Washington's most valuable assets was his six
feet and four inches. These men were perfect, physically.

We are exhorted in Scripture to attain unto "the
measure of the stature of the fullness of Christ." Jesus
was a perfect man physically. He was a man at his
climax. According to a description of His Personal
appearance read in the Senate chamber at Rome, He
was a model of physical beauty and perfection. Very
few have stopped to inquire as to His body. Was He tall
or short? Was He of full habit or aesthetic? Was He a
man of brawn or a weakling? Such questions would
formerly have been considered sacrilegious. But a
number of Scripture passages point to the humor of
Jesus; other passages teach that He was athletic, and it
is evident that He placed a premium upon a sound body
from the fact that He spent most of His time, when in
public, helping men physically.

Jesus was never sick. He lived the "simple life." He
breathed in the air of the open places. He kept close to
Nature. He was never in a hurry. Sickness means sin,

that is, broken laws, and we cannot think of Jesus as a sinner—"who knew no sin."

We should have more perfect men and women physically. With our advanced civilization; with the diffusion of sanitary knowledge and laws of life; sickness should be the exception, but alas! sickness is the rule.

There is a cult who teach that sickness should be abolished. This cult is "not far from the Kingdom."

We should employ our doctors to keep us perfectly healthwise. Now they simply come in to attempt to repair damages. The secret of the "healing art" should be the law of prevention. After a while, it will be the business of the physician to KEEP men well, rather than try to MAKE them well. The doctor of the future will be a teacher, rather than a practitioner; he will prescribe healthful ideas instead of pills. The Lord hasten the time.

The perfect man is an all-round man. However, perfect he may be in body, he will not neglect the best part of himself, his mind, his soul. The physical is the foundation. What is the building?

The etymology or word for man is suggestive. The Saxon Mon is "a one." Animals go in herds. He is a true man who can, whenever it is necessary, stand alone.

The Roman Vir, part of the word for virtue, was a hero on the field of combat. He only is a man, who is victor over himself and temptation.

The Greek Anthropos was "one who lifts up the eye." Brutes look down. The eye of guilt quails. The true man faces anything, man or God, time or eternity, without fear.

MAETERLINCK THINKS THAT THE CULTIVATION OF THE MANLY ART OF SELF-DEFENSE IS AN AID TO PEACE.

A friend of pugilism has appeared in an unexpected quarter. Maurice Maeterlinck, Belgian playwright, critic, and essayist, known as the Shakespeare of Belgium, has come forward with a defense of the "manly art." After pointing out that man is the most poorly equipped animal for defense or attack, he declares that among men the only weapon for purposes of protection, justice, and revenge should be the fist:

The study of boxing gives us excellent lessons in humility and throws a somewhat alarming light upon the forfeiture of some of our most valuable instincts. We soon perceive that in all that concerns the use of our limbs—agility, dexterity, muscular strength, resistance to pain—we have sunk to the lowest rank of the mammals, or batrachians. From this point of view, in a well-conceived hierarchy, we should be entitled to a modest place between the frog and the sheep.

The kick of the horse, the butt of the bull, the bite of the dog, are mechanically and anatomically perfect. It would be impossible to improve by the most learned lessons their instinctive manner of using their natural weapons. But we, the "hominians," the proudest of the primates, do not know how to strike a blow with our fist. We do not even know which exactly is the weapon of our kind.

Look at two draymen, two peasants, who come to blows; nothing could be more pitiable. After a copious and dilatory broadside of insults and threats they seize each other by the throat and the hair, make play with their feet, with their knees, at random, bite each other, scratch each other, get entangled in their motiveless rage, dare not leave go, and if one of them succeeds in releasing an arm he strikes out blindly and most often into space a series of hurried, stunted, sputtering little blows; nor would the combat ever end did not the treacherous knife, evoked by the disgrace of the incongruous sight, suddenly, almost spontaneously, leap from the pocket of one or the other.

On the contrary, watch two pugilists; no useless words, no gropings, no anger; the calmness of two certainties that know what lies before them. To the athletic attitude of the guard, one of the finest of the male body, logically exhibits all the muscles of the organism to the best advantage.

From head to foot, no particle of strength can now go astray. Each single one has its pole in one or other of the two massive fists charged to the full with energy. Three blows, no more, the fruits of secular experience, mathematically exhaust the thousand useless possibilities hazarded by the uninitiated. Three synthetic, irresistible, unimprovable blows.

It may seem paradoxical, but the fact is easily established that the science of boxing, in those countries where it is generally practiced and cultivated, becomes a pledge of peace and gentleness. Our aggressiveness, nervousness, our watchful susceptibility, that sort of perpetual state of alarm in which our jealous vanity moves, all these arise, at bottom, from the sense of our weakness and of our physical inferiority, which toil as best they may to overawe, by a proud and irritable mask, the men, often churlish, unjust, and malevolent, that surround us.

He who knows the source of justice which he holds in his two closed fists has no need for self-persuasion. Once and for al he knows; longanimity emanates like a peaceful flower from his ideal but certain victory. The grossest insult cannot impair his indulgent smile.

Peaceably he awaits the first act of violence, and is able to say to all who offend him: "Thus far shall you go and no farther." A single magic movement stops the insolence. Why make this movement? He ceases even to think of it, so certain is its efficacy.

———

Anchibald Maclaren, practically the founder of the modem gymnasium at Oxford University, and father of allied gymnastics in Great Britain, had this to say on the subject of exercise :

We are too prone, in this age when success seems to depend upon one's intellectual attainments, to feel that cultivation of the body implies a corresponding neglect of the brain; indeed, there are some so foolish as to wonder whether too great physical sturdiness does not stunt the brain. Science has proved conclusively that the most perfect development of the brain *depends absolutely* upon the sound, normal development of the body. It is true that there have been unusually great brains in very weak bodies—but how much greater would those brains have been had the bodies been fit to serve as running mates for the brains. "Even blind and blundering man," exclaims Mr. Maclaren, "does not yoke two oxen together to pull *against* each other. Mind and body can pull well together in the same team if the burden be fairly adjusted."

"In early boyhood and youth nothing can replace the active sports so much enjoyed at this period," writes Dr. John Keating; "and while no needless restrictions should be placed upon them, consideration should be paid to the amount, and especially to the character, of the games pursued by delicate youth. For these it would be better to develop the weakened parts by means of systematic exercises and by lighter sports."

"I am afraid there is a good deal more 'straining' than 'training' in a good many popular systems in vogue in the present day."

Maclaren has succinctly stated the three things that exercise accomplishes, in these words:

"It increases the size and power of the voluntary muscles employed.

"It increases the functional capacity of the involuntary muscles employed.

"It promotes the health and strength of the whole body by quickening circulation and increasing respiration."

Sydenham, one of England's great physicians, lay dying in 1860. Relatives, friends, and pupils stood about his bedside. They wept when he told them calmly that he was content to die, since he left behind him three physicians greater than he.

The bystanders looked at him in amazement. Could there be even one physician greater than the famous Sydenham?

One of the pupils questioned softly but wonderingly: "THREE! Who are they?"

Sydenham's dimming gaze roved over the faces of his hearers as he slowly replied:

"The three greatest physicians are AIR, WATER and EXERCISE."

A SQUARE

DEAL

GUARANTEE

IF AFTER sixty days Conscientious Trial under our Instruction, you do not feel fully benefitted and compensated for the outlay, on receipt of a letter of declaration from you to that effect in your hand writing, accompanied by the Chart and Letters of Instruction furnished by us, we will refund every dollar received from you. . . . . . .

Prof. F. S. Lewis
THE LEWIS SCHOOL
438 South Spring Street
LOS ANGELES, CALIFORNIA

Made in the USA
Las Vegas, NV
09 July 2021

26176221R00095